How To Get The D: Steps To Becoming A Doctor

DR. ASHLEY GILMORE

DEDICATION

I dedicate this book to my daughters, Amiya and Aubrey Gilmore. May you never let anyone define your success and you always seek opportunities to learn.

This book is a tool for all the beautiful ladies that were able to see their success once I obtained my doctorate degree, those that never imagined I could reach this monumental moment, and to the few that asked me what was next after graduation.

All of these women helped catapult me into the woman that I am today and I thank you! You played a part in me discovering my purpose upon graduating with my doctorate degree. May you discover your purpose and know that you can as well!

CONTENTS

INTRODUCTION

"You just got the job because you are a woman. I am more qualified than her! Why is she here?" These are all phrases that many women have heard once or twice, including myself. Due to this, women are required to work ten times harder to be able to experience career advancements and prove that they are just as capable, if not more capable than their peers.

Many of the people that said those words to me were women, but I attributed it to their discontentment with their position. However, when the men said it, I did not have those same feelings of discontentment. I began to self-doubt my status in life, comparing my past positions to my peers, and compartmentalize how much of my success was based on my expertise instead of my gender. As a young child, I was taught that women were malicious and men must protect women. How could a man in my life, that I saw as my protector say, "I got the job because I am a woman" and it not be true? I can recall hearing it from a male close to me and internalizing those words. I did not articulate the impact of those words, but those words pierced my skin, exposing layers of self-doubt that I never knew existed. Those words became my resume, not that I had the experience or was equipped in the knowledge. I knew that I was the subject matter expert in certain arenas, a powerful woman that could solve problems quicker than my peers, but I stood silent because I did not want to be sexualized.

There is power in discovering who you are as a woman, but also the strength that women possess. I could have chosen to continue letting other's words become my resume, but instead I decided to return their words back to them void. I understood that because of the positions in life I had achieved, my territory was being enlarged. When your territory is enlarged you must shift, deciding to create the resume for the position that you want. This forced me to project the best, authentic representation of myself. That meant that I would focus on how to get the "d", also known as degrees.

CHAPTER ONE:

Size Matters

"Do your research before you commit."

The first step towards getting prepared for another degree requires research. As a student, you must find the school that is best for your career goals. Never forget this step because it can cost thousands of dollars later if you decide to switch programs, worse schools. Accreditation within a college means everything! Not only are you checking to see if the college or university is accredited, but also the program that you are interested in.

Accreditation was created to ensure that all educational programs are following a set standard in training future leaders. However, if you decide to enter a program that is not accredited, financial aid will not assist in the costs for that program and many schools will not accept transfer credits if you decide to leave the program. There are some circumstances where students have been in a program that lost their accreditation and as long as they transferred within a certain period of time, their credits would still be accepted.

Remember, higher education is not the only way to be successful, but it provides a greater advantage in certain fields of work. When I was in high school, I was always told that as long as you have a high school diploma, you would be able to live the life you wanted. However, employers are starting to find the value behind higher education and for many jobs, they are requiring Master's degrees in order to have a high quality of life.

When I mention quality of life, it means being able to maintain a lifestyle that does not involve living paycheck to paycheck, but one that grants exposure to opportunities that will provide multiple streams of income. In reality, higher education is a tool that could allow people access to multiple streams of income. Many companies look within higher education student pools to offer top paying salaries to recent graduates. Secondly, there are great organizations on campus that can provide you with networking opportunities that could serve as great collaborations in your field of expertise.

The next step in searching for the right school to get your degree from is to decide whether you want to attend a for profit or non-profit school. Many for profit schools will have higher tuition rates, along with other slight differences from non-profit schools. There is no right or wrong here, but I will say that employers do look at the institutions you attended, although this does not make it right. When I selected my schools, I did not want any for profit schools, but I do know of individuals that have attended for profit schools and are excelling in their careers.

A step that many forget when selecting schools is also, researching the state that they plan on working in. Many professions have specific courses or degree plans that they will accept for certain professions. It would be frustrating to know that you received your degree and then have to take additional courses due to being unprepared for state requirements. If you switch programs in the process, always review state requirements!

Now here comes the hard question that you must answer, should you get an EdD or a PhD? At the end of the day, they both lead you to your doctorate, but it takes knowing what you are trying to accomplish to decide which degree is the best for you. When you tell people that you have your doctorate, the preconceived assumption is that it is a PhD, but there are other doctorate types. The EdD is for students that want to build knowledge within a particular discipline. Prior to the popularity of EdD degrees, many only knew PhD's, but jobs are more accepting of EdD degrees. However, PhD's are beneficial for students that are focused on research, so you must decide which degree path is right based on career aspirations.

The final step in considering my school was for me to research what professions was that school known for. For example, Harvard University is known for producing politicians and lawyers. It was best for me to find career professionals and understand the career paths that they took to get where they were. These professionals will serve as your model to follow. Going back to school, regardless of the degree or your age is a different learning process every time.

Just like an infant child learning to walk, "getting the d" can be very difficult. It is even more challenging if you add in being a daughter, sister, wife, mother, service member, and friend. However, these were all my titles and I understood early on that none of these titles could be neglected when I decided to go back to school. I was the person that people looked to for strength, so developing a comprehensive course of action to dominate every arena was a necessity.

CHAPTER TWO:

Protect Yourself

"Don't be afraid to ask questions, know your status"

It is my belief that in life, I must always be mindful of why things are done the way they are and their purpose for existing. If I do not fully understand the purpose behind things, then I tend not to give it my all. This is no different from when I started looking into going back to school for my doctorate. I had to ask myself, was I wanting to go back to school for the recognition? Maybe the money? Or just to prove to myself that I could do it.

I was on a great career path, so if I did not go back to school, that would have been fine at my present state of mind. However, after having my children I was forced to start planning for the next 15-20 years instead of just the present. I wanted my children to have a model of what a successful person looked like and let them understand that they could do anything if they focused on their goals. My goal in going back to receive my doctorate was to leave a legacy for my children and create generational wealth. In order to live the lifestyle, I desired, it required seeking gainful employment for adequate revenue.

With that being said, before I decided to go after my degree, I reflected on the purpose obtaining my degree would develop. By defining the purpose of why I wanted this degree, it helped me push through during the moments when I felt like giving up the most. There is nothing wrong with wanting your doctorate for the prestige that it brings, but understand that, a title without work is futile. So first, focus all efforts on discovering the purpose for applying to a doctoral program.

Daughter

I am the oldest daughter to Tuane Carr and Lisa Sellers (Banks), who calls Columbus, Georgia home after many military moves. By the time I graduated high school in Lithonia, Georgia, I had attended 15 schools. With attending that many schools, it is a given that I experienced many different obstacles along the way, but I never let them define me. Instead all of those moves made me stronger. In class every year, I received the comment that I was the most talkative, but I knew that I would be able to use my talking to my advantage. What others viewed as being disruptive, I viewed as understanding my environment and those immediately in it. Life is all about networking and having great communication skills, so I was already a step ahead by the time I was in the 3rd grade.

My parents always discussed the importance of education and

how in order to be great I must keep my head in the books. I can remember seeing the joy on my parent's face when I would say that I had excelled in my studies, even the times when I was so focused on being the model child until I wasn't. They never held any of that over my head, but reminded me that I was better than anything I thought and they expected me to excel. Every AB Honor Roll ceremony I had or scholarly recognition program, they were there supporting me. As the years passed, regardless of the many relationship strains, one thing always remained – my parents were proud of me. I knew that because of them, I had to continue to strive to let them see that their hard work was not in vain. That was my purpose as a daughter!

Sister

There is something about being a sibling that transforms you without you even fully comprehending. Whether older or younger, there is someone that will look up to you in certain areas. This journey to my doctorate was for my sister, but it was hard to excel while she was experiencing her own college hardships. While I was reaching milestones, she was at a plateau in her educational career and I did not understand how to be there for her and myself at the same time without considering her feelings. It is often hard to share your moments of joy or even issues, when the people who you want to share them with are going through hardships.

Those hardships that she experienced were some that many students along this journey will experience, but it made it hard because I understood that there was nothing I could do to make it easier for her. Later I realized that in those moments, I needed to share my successes and even the moments I was overwhelmed during my studies so that she could see how people overcame some of the same obstacles. When she wanted to give up, she looked at me and whether she continued because she did not want to let our parents down or maybe me – she continued. So my purpose as a sister was to let her see that she can do it and when she does, I will be there with the biggest smile to celebrate her.

Wife

Out of all of my titles, this area was the hardest one during my journey to my doctorate. Prior to starting my journey, I did not perform a proper appraisal over what would be sacrificed to obtain my doctorate. I understood the amount of time that I would have to allocate to assignments and research, but this also meant that there would be days when I would not have the energy to accommodate my husband. Whether that was cooking, cleaning, or simply just taking time to hear his heart about things on his mind. An appraisal of each area in your life will allow you to see how to fulfill every responsibility in your life based on the value that it has on your life.

The role of any significant other in your life is to be of support and encouragement, but sometimes that is hard to do when you both are excelling in different careers at the same time. By being cognizant of where you both are in life, it will develop a stronger appreciation for each other. In getting my doctorate, it allowed my husband to understand that he has a strong wife, who can be successful, funny, smart, but most importantly become the person that he needs each day as I strive to be the best for our family.

Mother

Being a mother to one child during school can be substantial, but when you are a mother to multiple children with busy schedules, that is when this journey gets even more challenging. Since the time my children have been of age to comprehend, I have been in school. However, I believe that by them seeing me complete my doctoral journey, they were able to see where they could be if they stay focused on their goals whether they decide to go to trade school or a 4 year institution.

With that being said, I have done my best to never miss an event in their life due to school. Were there events that I missed? Sure, but I planned things out so they never lacked my presence when they needed it the most. I believe this is something that I learned from my parents. My father worked night shift while I was in high school and it was just the two of us for a while, so our time was limited due to him having to provide. Due to this, he took one day out of every week to take me to breakfast before school and we would just talk. My mother would also leave during the middle of her work shifts to make events that I viewed as important, even if I only played for 3 minutes. I didn't understand why this was so important to them then, but now I do. It wasn't about what was said, but it was about them giving me time and letting me know that they were working hard to provide better for me and loved me.

The best advice I can offer in this journey is always being transparent in all areas of your life. I was always transparent with my children and because they were able to hear my heart, they were accepting of events that I could not attend. We capitalized on every moment we got together, even if it was a quick ice cream break. There were assignments that I did not do my best and even ones that I excelled, we celebrated every high and low together.

Transparency was important to me because I can remember the pressures I felt when school first started and not understanding that I did not have to be perfect. I did not understand that I could make mistakes and it created unnecessary pressures in my life. My purpose is to let my children have a model to follow in not just school, but life. They will make bad decisions, there will be assignments that they will not do well on, but they will not dwell on those moments for long. As my children, they will learn from the ups and downs of life and continue taking strides towards their purpose.

Service Member

I am American Airmen. I am a Warrior. – United States Air Force Airman's Creed

The first time I made the right decision in my life after losing my scholarship to college was when I joined the United States Air

Force. It was one of those decisions where I knew that I had to find a way to afford school and I wanted to be able to financially not depend on family. It has truly been one of the best decisions I could ever have made. I finished my Bachelor's while living in Okinawa, Japan, my Masters while deployed overseas, and experienced multiple assignments while completing my doctorate.

Being a member in the military provides you a guaranteed job, but many who join the military do not always retire. It is the same on the civilian side with jobs. We create lasting friendships with our co-workers and then they decide to leave to find a better job. My purpose in this degree was to implant a vision of more into those that I worked with. Plans are ever changing and even those that considered the military being their only option, for some reason or another they were unable to continue their journey.

Not only will your degree form a more marketable resume in regard to your experience, but it will also let you be an inspiration. Your co-workers will pull on you for support and strength to push them to greater.

Friend

As my mother use to say, "be careful who you call a friend". However, everyone needs 2-3 good friends who they can call during their times of need. Whether one is the friend that is good for lunch dates to take a break from reality, or the friend that is the encourager to keep pushing you late at night when you are working, or the friend that can handle everything from life, family, and school issues. For me, I am the friend that handles everything, so when I entered school I discussed it with my friends. I understood the importance of having my friends there for me and them being able to understand that I would need more from them during my doctorate journey.

While I was thinking of the purpose of getting this degree as it pertained to my friends, I realized it was to motivate my friends. Within all circles of friends, there should always be forward progress. If I am doing the best out of my friends then I need new friends because I do not want to become stagnant. When I completed my doctorate, my friends were there supporting me through the whole way. The nights when I called crying because I lost a paper and had to turn it in late, the time I failed a class, and even the times when I just needed to sip a tall glass of wine and talk about life.

Throughout this journey, we all changed for the better. Those closest to me went back to school, prepped to study for their MCAT, and even received promotions at work. I ignited the fire back in their lives to gather their dreams and continue. It was so easy to get complacent with where we were because we were all successful, but real friends are like a seesaw. Seesaws are made to elevate people, friends must be prepared to lift their friends up during low moments and help their friends see higher than they currently are seeing.

CHAPTER THREE:

Give it to Me

"There is more than one way to get what you want"

It would be absurd to think getting a doctorate degree would be inexpensive, due to this many students retreat from even applying. Let me reassure you that getting a doctorate without having to pay much, if anything is possible! I repeat, IT IS POSSIBLE! The problem is, people have been told for so long that student loans are the only way to get it done and the fear of debt prevents people from trying. While student loans are great for assisting in higher education, they should be your last resort. One of the greatest opportunities that we have as students looking into doctorate programs are fellowships.

Fellowships are essentially scholarships for doctorate students.

The best option is to research the program that you want to study and then search for fellowships throughout the country if you are able to relocate. If you are unable to relocate then you have a decision to either continue to wait on a fellowship near you or find other options to afford school. The best thing to do is find other options instead of waiting because if you continue waiting, the right time to go back will never occur.

Some options are setting out time in your week to develop a regimen for applying to scholarships. A good regimen that I tell people to do is to apply for a minimum of 3 scholarships a week. In order to become successful at scholarship searching you must create a spreadsheet or tracking plan to record all the scholarships of interest, deadlines, and requirements needed. By creating the spreadsheet with all of that information, you will then be able to structure your month appropriately to maximize the number of scholarships you can apply to. Another great tip in regards to scholarships that I have learned is to apply for scholarships that you already have essays prepared for the specific topic they are requesting.

Many scholarships will ask for essays that discuss who you are, overcoming adversity, or how their agency has assisted you or your family. Keep these thoughts in mind when searching for scholarships. This will increase your chances of securing funding; it is also good to increase engagement with certain organizations for funding. Social media has created a platform that allows organizations to share their scholarships and target certain students that match their criteria. Locate organizations that align with your studies and apply to their scholarships.

In order to be successful at receiving scholarships, you must be aggressive in your search. Scholarship searching is like fishing, you cast out your line with bait, which would be scholarship applications and after you have sent out so much bait, eventually you get a catch. Your scholarship that you catch may not be the biggest, but you must focus on the goal. If you are unable to get any scholarships, there is always the option of loans as well. The best way to be considered for loans outside of your banking institutions is through completing your Free Application for Federal Student Aid (FASFA). This application will allow you to see how much financial assistance the Department of Education will provide for your studies.

Instead of loans, I decided to use the benefits earned through the military because I could not do a fellowship and maintain my military obligations. Let me be clear for those military members wondering how did I stretch 36 months of the Post 9/11 into my program, this took planning and determination. I entered the military knowing that I was going to receive my degrees, so I started out with Tuition Assistance and grants to complete my Bachelors degree. When it was time for my Masters degree, my mother had been awarded 100% disability through the military and the state of Alabama had options for free schooling to her children.

I say that to say, please look into your state of residency for scholarships for veterans, military members, and any other options that you qualify for.

It was my plan to use my Post 9/11 educational benefits for my doctorate, but after my mother got her 100% disability through the military, I was able to use Ch. 35 benefits to complete my degree. This took me staying proactive and knowing what benefits I was entitled to and networking with the right agencies.

The final thing that many students do not think of, is reviewing the educational benefits that their jobs offer. Many jobs offer their employees educational benefits as soon as 6 months into working within the company. With that being said, there are limitations to what they will pay based on degree plans and other factors but check into it. If you are lackadaisical in searching for financial assistance, you will also become lackadaisical on completing your doctoral degree. This is no small feat, ensure that you want to obtain your degree before potentially giving yourself unnecessary debt. Lastly, the school that you are attending usually offers additional scholarship opportunities outside of fellowships, so apply to them as well. Remember, you must stay persistent in the journey to secure funding.

CHAPTER FOUR:

Take it Slow

"Learn how to set up the mood and take your time."

The first thing many prospective students ask me once they know I have been in school is how many courses did I take and do I recommend terms or semesters for school. First, my personal preference is to take my courses through terms instead of semesters, although I have done both due to the schools that I attended. Taking your classes on terms requires more focus, but the end result is being able to maximize the amount of courses that you are able to take and ultimately graduate sooner. Secondly, the first term or semester with any program I recommend only taking 2 classes max, in order to allow yourself time to get back into the structure of school.

Often times the excitement and prestige of being a college student consumes our minds and we overload our first term or semester with more than we can handle. Sometimes slow is better than fast, there is no need to rush the courses. In order to figure out what works best for you, there are a few things to consider. First, will you have the time to take more than one class at a time? Are there any previous courses that you took in your previous studies that can count towards your degree? Is there a certain time all of your classes must be done, due to funding constraints?

I found it best to take 2 courses at a time, but I did have some classmates that took 3-4 at a time. When you decide how many classes that you need to take, also consider your projected timeline to complete your degree, but remember that this is just a plan and plans are meant to change. Based on the timeline that I had in order to prevent myself from paying out of pocket due to my GI Bill, I took 2 courses at a time, which allowed me to complete my program within 3 years. For some, this was a very challenging timeline with a busy family schedule, but I did not want my educational benefits to run out. Find what works best for you and STICK WITH IT!

Plan the courses that you take strategically! If you have courses on your degree plan that focus on similar if not the same subjects, it is always best to take those classes simultaneously. This will decrease the number of hours you will spend researching for assignments, due to all of your assignments being focused on the same topics. Be mindful that all classes should build on each other and become more targeted on your dissertation or capstone research.

Another best practice to monitoring your course load is to print out a degree plan evaluation. This is merely a breakdown of all of the course requirements for your degree and the order that the school recommends your courses be taken. When you print out your degree plan evaluation, take a pencil and write which semesters or terms you will take the courses on this evaluation. This will allow you to see the projected end goal of when you will complete your degree, be mindful this date is only tentative. Throughout your journey there will be semesters or terms when a course may not be available or another reason that may shift your timeline, but you are still taking the steps to reach your goal.

Lastly, when reviewing your course load, make sure during registration you pick teachers that engage your learning style. The worst thing you can do is have a full course load and then experience a teacher that does not work with your learning style. If this is neglected, this will cause you to make careless mistakes and your purpose of school will begin to be tested. You will wonder if you have made the right decision to enroll in school because your frustrations will overpower your purpose.

Once you begin in your program, be prepared to have at least 2 papers due a week in the 8-15 page range. This will be a common paper requirement for the next 3-6 years of your program. The question you must factor into your course load is, are you able to handle 8-15 page papers, work, life, and family with that schedule. When you discover what works best for you, do not change. There will be friends you meet along your program that will persuade you to shift your structured plan, but you must remain grounded or risk being setback in your plans.

CHAPTER FIVE:

How You Like It

"Not everyone can handle this the way you do"

This journey to the "d" requires you to have a heart to heart with yourself. I found myself saying multiple times, "Ashley, why do you keep doing this to yourself?" Every week I kept waiting until the last minute to do assignments, but honestly, that was what worked for me. One time in particular, I was exhausted from a long week and waited until 7 that night to work on a paper that was due by midnight. I knew that typing papers was easy for me and my best work was under pressure. They say, "Diamonds are created under pressure", so why couldn't my masterpieces be created under pressure as well? However, this one time, I fell asleep during the last hour and woke up to all of my work erased. I learned two things that night; never sip a particular brand of wine because it puts me to sleep and the power of holding the control key and then pressing the letter s to save my work.

At the end of the day, everyone is not the same as me so do not take my mindset, unless you know yourself! I suggest discovering what you're learning style is prior to the start of your second semester. The first semester into your program, you should be gaining an understanding of the university's policies, procedures, and different teaching styles. One benefit of being in a doctoral program is that you will have the same teachers for most of your program and they will sit on your committee board for your dissertation or capstone. Be mindful for how responsive the teachers are not only to emails, but also during class with them. If you find yourself confused more times than not, then it may be the teacher's style of teaching and that's a teacher whose classes you do not need to take.

Although teacher's styles of teaching could be an issue, it could be your learning style that needs to be considered as well. There are many great assessments you can take to understand your learning style, but by this point in your educational endeavors, you should be well aware of your learning style. As a visual learner, there were many times during my studies that I had to ask for examples on what my instructors were requiring. When I first started my program, I was afraid to ask for visuals because I did not want to be a "high maintenance" student, but this did not last long. As a student, you are paying teachers for their services to accommodate and instruct you, so simply put ASK EVERYTHING!

Visual learners like myself, thrive off of examples and thorough instructions. Instructors have examples for every assignment that students are required to complete, so never feel embarrassed to ask for an example if you do not comprehend assignments. When you get further into your studies, the charts and tables that are required for your research must be a certain way and it is easier to see an example.

It is also beneficial to print out the class syllabus and create a weekly schedule of assignments that need to be done. Once you have completed the assignments, cross them out so you can reprioritize tasks that need to be completed based on their level of importance. There is never a free week during your doctoral journey, even if it is holiday break. Research can and must always be conducted, even if it is just reviewing one article aligned with your research topic.

For the students that are more auditory learners, you have a gift! I never have been one to just hear something and be able to understand everything fully. This student is one that will need to know their professor's office hours and have routine office visits or weekly phone conferences. It is your responsibility to stay on top of your professor and ask the right questions to get your work done. It is also helpful to have a classmate that learns differently than you, so you both can review the assignments from a different perspective and compare information.

CHAPTER SIX:

Enjoy the Ride

"Close your eyes, cry, or scream, either way it's almost over"

Breathe, look at what you have accomplished up until this point, and know that you are meant to be where you are at this very moment. There will be moments where you cry due to the stress whether it is finances, grades, or misconceptions of a strong support system, but enjoy the ride. All of these moments of doubt will mean nothing when you receive your degree. The nights being frustrated with people for not understanding your absence from events will become irrelevant.

You have to wake up every day affirming that you will be the best subject matter expert in your study. I remember being scared to tell people that I was getting my doctorate because I knew that others would hold me accountable and push me to get my doctorate degree. I thought, what if I don't finish? What if I bit off more than I can chew? All of these questions on top of not being around the right people to encourage me and speak into my life were weighing heavy on me. Then one day, something clicked inside of me and my fear left me. As soon as I told those closest to me and shared it to my social media, not only did the fear leave, but also in place was support.

During my program, there were assignments that I needed feedback from people and a simple social media post got me the necessary information. Then when I needed to interview certain people based on their job titles, social media was able to connect me again. Every moment that I initially had doubt, I realized that without social media I would have self-sabotaged my success if I did not remove doubt and ask for assistance. There were more people in my corner cheering me on simply for being young, black, a mother, or simply put for being a woman. I let other women see that they could do the same thing I was doing; especially those women that looked just like me.

It is important that you get around like minded individuals and they do not all have to be going to school for a doctorate degree, but they must have the mindset for success. The more that they discuss success; the more it becomes engrained into your thoughts and strengthens you. I would reflect over all of the past classes I took and how difficult I thought the classes were while I was enrolled, but I was able to complete them all. Then I had my daughters looking up to me always asking me two questions that I often asked them, so that they would think about their actions before they would do anything. They asked me, who am I and who do I represent?

Well, the answer was a simple response I had instilled into them daily, so that if anyone ever told them differently, they would not lower their standards to believe it. I was a beautiful, black, talented, and smart woman. I represented God, Jesus, and my parents. I could not let doubt sink into my life because I had people listening to me and expecting me to overcome.

Doubt cannot be removed until you replace it with reasons why you can complete whatever task is facing you. Whether you have to focus on your purpose, the stress relieved from completing it, or any other reason, just replace the doubt in your life. My replacement was increasing daily affirmations over my life and looking at the career professional models I first found when looking into what program to study. Many of them shared how they were not the best academically, but that did not stop them from overcoming challenges and that was encouraging.

Another outlet for me to remove doubt was sharing my journey with the people that wanted to see me make it, so that I could empower other people by telling my story. The doubt still arose when I did not do my best in my classes, but I did not let it consume me because I understood that I had a greater purpose. Just like anything in life, you are always tested right when you seem to be on top, so never grow complacent.

During my 4th semester in school, I got complacent in a class and received a C. Many are taught or have heard, "C's get degrees", but when getting your doctoral degree, C's do not get degrees. A C is equivalent to an F in doctoral programs and I was forced to retake the class, risking the possibility of having to pay out of pocket to retake the course. I was frustrated because the teacher would not give me extra credit and I knew that I could have done better, but I took the class for granted because I was excelling in my studies until that point.

Looking back, I am glad that she did not give me extra credit in the class because if I am honest with myself, school until that point was easy. I would wait until the last minute to write papers, I wasn't challenged much, and I needed something to shake me in order to make me appreciate the opportunity in front of me. At the same time, doubt started to creep back because I was disappointed that I took this opportunity for granted. Not only that, but I was concerned because I felt as if I let those looking up to me down.

Then it hit me, if I quit because I failed, then I would be letting those looking up to me down. Everyone will fail at some point in his or her life, but as long as you do not stay down, it simply becomes a lesson that you learned. I told doubt that there was no place in my space for it and focused hard on passing the class. The one great thing about failing the class was that the teacher whose class I failed, was teaching the same class the following semester. I decided to take her class again because in reality, it was an easy class; I just had to apply myself. I knew the assignments and she worked with me, so I was able to submit a few of the same assignments again. By her doing this, I was able to focus on the assignments that I knew would demand more from me.

After passing that class, I promised that I would start to enjoy the journey to my doctorate degree and fully apply myself. This journey was a stressful one, but there were some positives to enjoy including friendships developed, the funny stories I got to share with my kids about my presentations, and being able to enjoy life. There were some weekends when I would miss going out with friends and family, but for the most part, I still enjoyed my life including the doctoral journey.

CHAPTER SEVEN:

Threesomes

"Understand your desires and be selective on who can give them"

There will always be a tier of people in your life that will advise you, whether it is school, work, or relationships. For me, my tier had three levels and included my family, friends, and advisors. Every decision I made in my program, I had to bounce them off of my family, friends, and advisors. Let me be clear, this did not involve all of my family, friends, and advisors.

When I looked into my family, I had to find the one or two family members that I knew I could trust and that had the capacity to be there for me. Some family members are not able to handle your pressures from school because they have their own issues. They will seem to be listening, but you will be able to tell quickly if they retained the information. Or they would not be able to keep my personal moments to themselves. The one thing you can never do when finding the right people to be a part of your tier is to take anything personal.

I knew early on, who in my family would be my tier person and I stuck with her. It would prove to be of extreme importance when I lost my site for my research and she helped find another site for me. The purpose of the tier is to get the assistance you need whether it is advice or merely connections. For every 1-2 people in each level of your tier, you are connecting yourself to 3-6 more people per tier. This is vital in order to get the resources needed to complete your program.

Everything about your tier and your program selection is intentional. If you are in the educational career field, then keep educators in your tier or those that have experience and can offer feedback from different perspectives. My family member was a counselor within the school system, so I knew that she could understand my research interests as well as guide me with some assignments if I needed assistance. The one thing to remember when going after your doctorate degree is that you will not have all of the answers. I relied on her to be able to provide me with encouragement, advice, and the resources to complete my program.

The one friend that I allowed into my tier had received her Masters and offered great input on methods to complete my studies. She was going through her own decisions with school, so she understood the issues I was experiencing. Not only was school her area of expertise, but being a wife as well. There were moments when I felt that I was being forced to choose between school and my marriage, but she helped me understand how to change my perspective on situations I was experiencing and give attention to both areas equally.

Without me trusting that she had the best interests for my family, I may have either quit school or my marriage. It took many late night conversations of reminding me why I decided to go back to school and the importance of my family to get me through my doctorate degree. This does not mean that my friends who were not in school could not be as beneficial, but I shared more information with her because she offered me experiences that were relatable. Lastly, it is best to develop a one on one relationship with your advisor.

An advisor's role is to provide information that can help you make the best decision for your life. There are advisors within colleges and universities, but sometimes it is a great idea to have an advisor outside of school as well. There were 3 advisors that I kept during my studies, one to direct my research and the others to direct me personally. My field advisor was someone that had longevity in the education field and was very passionate about providing higher education resources to minorities. She worked at the local community college and served on multiple initiatives to assist with first generation students being accepted to college. Through multiple conversations, she single-handedly selected my research topic.

I remember going to lunch with her and showing her all the titles/topics that I was interested in and I waited for her opinion on every topic. Notice I did not say, "I went in to tell her these were my topics and why". When seeking someone's assistance, you must humble yourself and listen to what they have to say. It would be insulting to ask her to lunch so that I can seek her wisdom on my topics and then not allow her the opportunity to share due to my own insecurities. So, I watched her review all of my topics and she shared which topics had more research for me to be successful and which areas she had more knowledge in. In that moment, I knew that I made the right decision having her as my advisor.

In regards to my personal advisors, they advised me on all things outside of school. This person could be a counselor, therapist, life coach, or pastor. By having a personal advisor, you are able to become more vulnerable with things that you are experiencing, but too ashamed to tell your friends due to not wanting to appear vulnerable. I needed this person to let me just say, "I'm tired!" and let me have that moment. There were times when I just wanted to be in my feelings for a while and not be pushed. It felt good to be able to have my moment and then we would go eat and talk about everything except school. However, at the end of every conversation they would remind me that I would finish school and they understood I was tired. Everyone's main goal, regardless of their category was to simply help me prioritize and make the best decision for my goals.

CHAPTER EIGHT:

Climb on Top

"No one can get you there better than you can"

Being on top allows you to look at everything that you have completed and see things that still need your attention. There will be many times during your studies that you will feel like you are on top and then, something shifts your balance. In order to remain on top, you must first understand who you are before you even enter the program. Also understand that you must take care of your mind, body, and soul.

Throughout the duration of your program, never be afraid to take time out for just you. Since I have begun college, I have always been a wife and then my second year of college, I added being a mother. The one thing I found to work best for me was taking time for me. Become unapologetic about needing time for yourself. There will be times when you have plans with others, but you do not have to make everything. I took frequent trips throughout my time in school, even if it was just a 2-hour drive away from home and relaxing near the water. You have to be selfish sometimes in your program and understand that every sacrifice you make now will pay double in prosperity in the future.

When entering this program, create a regimen in your week where you dedicate time to provide attention to your mind, body, and soul. If you neglect one area, it will create an imbalance requiring other areas to work harder until you burn out. Also remember to drink plenty of water. Water not only is healthy for you, but it keeps your skin clear and you can feel good about yourself. It is important to never let yourself go physically. Even on your worse days, get dressed and talk back to your bad day. Speak positivity into your day and never let anyone in your environment that does not put your mind, body, and soul first.

One practice to stimulate your mind is through reading, meditation, and believe it or not social media. When used properly, social media can become a resource to stimulating information. Find social media pages that have individuals on the same career path or at the same institution. This was very helpful for me to connect with people that took the classes I was in and provide insight on best practices for the classes.

The insight that they gave allowed me to prepare myself for the class mentally, readjust things so I would be able to optimize my time in school, and also encouraged me during my program. It created a sense of community that could relate and when I would have an issue pertaining directly to the school I attended, they knew how to get quick results due to them attending the same school. This provided me the peace of mind that was needed to bring balance.

In order to stay connected to your body while in school, you must find what works best for you. I turned to running at least once a week to create an outlet of alone time, but also forcing my body to reach a point of exhaustion. Some of the best rest that I received during my time in college was after a good workout because I was so exhausted physically, that my mind was forced to shut down and I could not think or worry about my studies.

It was also necessary for me to take care of my body after pushing it to a point of exhaustion. I began scheduling monthly massage appointments into my schedule so that I could release any toxins trapped in my body and relieve stress. This was also designated time that forced my mind and body to relax due to the environment. I was also able to block out any unwanted conversations that I felt obligated to responding to if I was contacted because massages forced me to put my phone down.

The spiritual component of balance was the hardest for me to do. Being spiritually balanced involves slowing your mind down and seeking understanding. As a full-time student, full-time worker, mother, wife, and many other titles, slowing down was not in my picture. I thrived off of being around people and being able to connect with my friends. However, the balance required for the spiritual component involved me sitting in silence, disconnected from all distractions to hear from God.

I needed Him to encourage me during situations that I did not share with others on my journey. I also needed to become one with learning more about who I was becoming and the things that I did and did not like. The best way for me to do this was to journal about how I felt, where I saw myself, and things that brought me peace. By becoming aware of who I was and what I needed, I was able to identify things that did not align with me spiritually, quicker and prevent disruption later in my studies.

CHAPTER NINE:

Favorite Position

"Sometimes it's not about what others want, be selfish"

Here is the fun part of the whole process to becoming a doctor, but it will be the most stressful as well, outside of completing comps, depending on your program requirements. From the beginning of your doctorate journey, you should have been developing the target for your topic and have a catalog of articles that you will use for your dissertation or capstone. Your topic must have a measurable problem that can be addressed through your research. Ensure that your topic is also specific and not a generalized topic. For example, instead of focusing on graduation rates, make your topic be on low graduation rates. The key is making your targeted research more specific.

At this point in your journey, you will be assigned a mentor or committee to assist you in writing your dissertation or capstone. It is vital to ensure that your mentor or committee has the same interest as your study. If they do not have the best interest in mind for your study then you have to advocate for your study. Your mentor or committee has the final say not only on your topic, but also on your research outside of the IRB process. They will be able to steer your research and collaborate with you on different perspectives to approach for your study.

Once you have been paired with a mentor or committee that is conducive to your study, you must turn in your finalized topic to them for approval. Each university has a template on how they want the topic to be developed along with the timeline for how their process goes, but the key is never skipping steps in the topic development phase.

The best practice is to locate an issue once you have identified your site. Your site will be the basis of where all your research will be conducted, whether that is a school, hospital, or another business. Identifying your site will then pinpoint the participants that will be researched. When my program started, I had identified a site that I knew possessed substantial data in academia for me to compare during my research. Secondly, my field advisor and I had already developed my topic, so the foundation was created for me to develop a title and questions that would guide my research and prepare to defend my topic before my chair. The overwhelming nerves grew the closer it came to defend my topic, but then I remembered that I was the expert in the route I wanted my research to go. I discussed in great detail my topic, the importance of my research, and elaborated on questions from my chair.

I got the approval to continue my topic after my defense, but it is important that I share I did not get approved the first 2 times I went forward with my topic. The debate on whether I should begin data collection without approval plagued my mind because I knew in my heart that my research was needed in the topic that I had decided upon. However, do not do this because it could affect you negatively whether it is IRB disapproval or being dismissed from your program. Instead, I worked overtime to correct the necessary areas and after 2 weeks, I got approval to pursue my topic.

Once you receive approval on your topic, the true work begins. You must stay in constant communication with the site where your research will be conducted and begin coordinating the schedule for you to conduct interviews and focus groups, if your study calls for that. It is helpful to send over all consent forms and overview information of your study prior to scheduling anything because it allows your targeted population or group time to be able to prepare.

Interviews can be the best part of your journey due to you being in the field or it can be the hardest. This part of my journey was a bit of both due to the population that I was using for my survey. In regards to the interview and focus groups, faculty and staff within my site were used, but the surveys had to come from students. When it comes to getting survey results depending on how long the surveys are, you may have to create an incentive to complete the surveys. It is a good idea to conduct your research for 2 weeks without incentive, but if you notice that you are still behind in collecting data then offer gift cards.

Gift cards are the perfect touch to get someone to participate in a survey. The surveys do not require much effort, students just do not want to take the time out of their schedules due to other obligations they have. However, all college students could use gift cards and you do not have to provide gift cards to every participant if your funds are tight. One way to do the gift cards is by creating a random drawing system and after every 5th student to complete the survey; a name will be called from the group of students.

Once you have noticed that you have collected a sufficient amount of data, you must communicate that with the site director. The site director must be made aware of all progress with the study and remain in constant contact to ensure that you are abiding by the site's rules and also out of respect. You want the site director to understand how important of a role they played in your success with your doctoral degree. This degree is not one that you will get on your own; everyone that you connect with along the way will have a vital role that they will play as well.

After all of the data has been collected, you must then discover how you are going to explain your results. For my study, I focused on the themes that kept repeating themselves in my study based on the interviews, focus group, and survey responses. Once the themes were identified, I had to determine the best method to visually show my findings. My findings were annotated in a chart and then further discussed throughout my manuscript. However, I was not prepared for what was to come next.

CHAPTER TEN:

Rounds

"One time is never good enough, prepare for more."

Imagine defending your proposal topic, getting approval to begin your research, conducting all of your research, and presenting all of your research just to be told that you did not do enough. It doesn't matter the hours that you sacrificed away from your family, the meals you missed caused you were focused on your research, or loss of sleep because it still was not enough. That is how edits feel each and every time you have to submit them!

The final classes leading up to your dissertation or capstone classes, your only focus is on your rough draft and then when you begin collecting data you are just adding to the previous sections that professors approved. However, every professor's preference is obsolete once you have your chair or mentor. This was a tough pill for me to swallow because I went from getting my chapters 1-2 approved, to now having my manuscript torn apart. Round 1 of edits, my title was changed 2 times to become more specific, I went from using APA 6 to APA 7 being introduced, and losing 10 references due to their information being outdated.

So besides sipping a lot of wine, I had to figure out how to overcome edits. In order to overcome edits it required a 3-part system, which I implemented and recalled by the acronym F. – I.T.

Follow-Up - Intake Tackle

I would be lying if I said that after I received my edits I literally did not want to scream "f-it!" but I understood that would not change anything.

Instead, I understood that edits were a way for me to be able to take the feedback received and follow up for understanding on better ways to guide my research. The follow up phase also provided me one on one time with my mentor to help me dig deeper to understand higher education. She was able to share her experiences in higher education and I was able to ask further questions in developing my research.

Another great benefit from my edits was that I was able to utilize more of the resources offered through my school to locate more research on my topic. This was the intake phase, during this phase a plan is created to process the edits and feedback received from your mentor or chair and task assignment begins. Yes, it was a hassle to have to redo my research but I realized later that I was not properly utilizing my resources offered through my school. My research was building off of past researchers and I needed to ensure that I fully conveyed the timeline of past research to stress the importance of my research.

Once this was done, it was my responsibility to ensure that I comprehended everything, in order to tackle my manuscript. My mentor was available for every question that I had along the way, but only if I reached out to her. I understood that she wanted me to become the best researcher, but she was not there to just push my research through because she saw my potential. Her name was on my manuscript and she was apart of my success as if it was hers as well, so when I realized we were a team instead of her being an enemy, my research became easier.

There were no timelines on when edits were due back to my mentor, however the longer that I waited, the longer my time of completing my degree was being pushed back. I made it my point to give myself 9 days to complete all edits and not a day over. Usually when I got my edits back, I would spend the first day analyzing the edits, thinking of ways to attack the edits, and then just relaxing because I knew the next few days would be mentally tough for me. Day two of edits, would be me making the minor corrections she would find like spacing and anything that I signified as an easy correction. The rest of the days were focused on researching and correcting all major edits. I believe this system allowed me not to become overwhelmed with edits and also maintain my optimistic outlook in regards to my degree.

Another thing that allowed me to get through edits was developing an accountability partner within my program. This person does not take away from your tier people, but compliments your tier of supporters. The one benefit about this accountability partner is that they are in the same program as you and generally on the same round of edits. You want your accountability partner to be someone that has strength in an area that you are weak in. For me, my accountability partner was proactive in explaining the things within the course that I could not grasp. We also were able to share things to correct during the edits prior to submitting it.

Being able to make corrections to your edits prior to submitting them for review with your chair or mentor can be vital to your timeline. With each round of edits, you must allow a 2-week turnaround for your work because lets face it; you are not the only doctoral student in pursuit for their doctorate degree. So maximize the relationship of your accountability partner through encouraging each other, sharing pertinent information in order for each other to be successful, and also share a laugh with each other.

Another thing that you should be working on during the down

time from edits is updating your resume and networking with professionals that are in the field you want to enter in after you finish your degree. Depending on when you graduate, there may be new career opportunities available based on being in the right place at the right time and knowing the right people. Also, take the time to compare your resume to people that are in the field you want to be in, so you understand how to format your resume.

Lastly, find the time to enjoy the 2 weekends of freedom that comes with edits. The edit process can take a toll on your mind and if you do not develop a good time management system then areas in your life suffer. During this freedom, it is the perfect time for you to re-evaluate your progress in your doctoral journey and immediate areas that you deal with daily to include work, family, and church to ensure effective time management systems. When you are re-evaluating your progress in each area, you are monitoring to see if anything has been overlooked and what methods have worked best for you to be successful. The doctoral journey is just one journey out of many that you will experience, so you can implement the same methods that worked for your doctoral journey on other journeys, hence the importance of re-evaluation in everything that you do in life.

CHAPTER ELEVEN:

Climax

"This is what you have been waiting for, show them what you got"

Now comes the fight of your educational career. This is the fight that you have dreamed of all those late nights staying up doing homework, missed events, and nights of uncertainty. In this moment, you must stay focused, encouraged, and remember that you are the subject matter expert of your research. There is no one that knows your research better than you do and if you remember this then you will get through this monumental moment.

Defending your research is as much mental as it is physical. With that being said, trust in your research and understand that your mentor or chair would not let you defend if they felt you were not ready. The best preparation methods that worked for me was to rehearse my presentation, pick the best outfit, and limit my distractions. On this day, I did not concern myself with anyone's emergencies and you must be cognizant of this as well. Throughout my whole doctoral journey, I was the strong person for my family, but this one-day was my day of selfishness. I placed my phone on do not disturb, ate my favorite feel-good snacks, and listened to gospel music. It was everything I needed to set the tone for my success. It is vital that you learn to become unapologetically selfish in certain circumstances; ignoring your phone, canceling appointments, and eliminating anything that does not bring peace.

Rehearsing my presentation allowed me to ensure that all my research was covered, all transitions between subjects were smooth, and time requirements were met. It is best to rehearse your presentation at least 3 times, making sure to have an audience at least one time. By allowing an audience to witness your presentation, they will be able to provide effective critiques on ways to improve your presentation before you defend.

I was told from a young age "if you look good then you feel good." Everyone has a color that compliments their skin tone the best, so that is the color that you want to wear on your defense day. This will exuberate confidence and let your mentor or chair see that you came prepared to defend. The last thing to bring to your physical appearance is your smile. Even if you do not feel that your presentation is going well, smile through it because your mentor or chair does not know how nervous you are.

Now that you have rehearsed your presentation and found the right outfit, it is time to defend. Arrive early for your presentation so that you can troubleshoot any technological issues with your presentation, this will also give you time to control the environment that you are in. When you defend, it may be in a location that you are not familiar with, so it will ease your nerves being able to understand the layout of your environment. This is also the perfect time for you to pray prior to everyone arriving and set the atmosphere for success.

Be prepared for your mentor or chair to start the defense with ice breaker questions, after all your mentor or chair was in the same position you are currently in so they understand the nerves. Their goal is to ease your mind, but also ensure that you have earned your degree as a researcher. While giving your presentation, stand tall with your shoulders pushed back and control your presentation, making sure to take slow breathes to calm your nerves. After your presentation, there should be zero boxes unchecked in regards to if you are ready to enter the field. However, be prepared for 1-3 questions in regards to your presentation or suggestions about how your research can be applied when you enter the field. Then they will say your name!

CHAPTER TWELVE:

Say My Name

"You know it's good when they say your name"

"Congratulations, Dr. Ashley Gilmore!" Those words made my world stop, I wanted to scream, but I still had to remain professional, after all I was still receiving feedback based on my presentation. All throughout your program, you envision how that moment will be and the littlest things that do not matter. For instance, how to write your signature block at work and what others will think about a 29 year old African American woman receiving such a prestigious degree.

During the rest of the formalities from my presentation, I could not wait to leave and share the news with those closest to me. As soon as my presentation was over, I went and told my husband and daughters. It meant everything for me to share this joy with my daughters because I understand that my responsibility is to show them things I never got to experience, with expectations that they will be greater than the example I have set. With her beautiful brown eyes and the biggest hug I can remember feeling, my youngest daughter looked at me and said, "Congratulations Dr. Mommy, Ashley Gilmore!" Then came the joy and excitement from my husband and oldest daughter. The last few months felt like I would never see the end and I remember telling my classmate that I was over it and he never let me quit. Instead he shared his progress and then we would discuss our next steps until we could be complete.

Once the excitement was over, the countless emails about what to do in order to graduate began to start filling my inbox. Although I passed my defense, it was not official until my transcript stated, "degree conferred". This took 2 weeks to become conferred and once it was, I was officially able to submit the necessary documentation within my organization for pay increases and more responsibilities. Secondly, I wanted to begin searching for adjunct positions to secure my plans for life after military retirement.

This degree will expose you to many different environments, but always remember that it should not change the level of respect that you have for others. Many become a doctor and then lose themselves in titles. Respect is given, just because you have the title doctor before your name, it does not give you permission to become obnoxious. Now, there is a time and place when it is acceptable to display your credentials, but character determines how far a person can go in the world, not titles. As a doctor you will be trusted with more responsibilities, but you need members on a team to help you be successful. You will be able to have more people help you and stay to see you meet all your goals based on character.

The moment I knew that I made a difference was when people would introduce me as Dr. Ashley, instead of me doing it. I did not have to announce myself because there were people around me that were proud of my success and refused to let me settle. Whether they called me Ashley or Dr. Ashley, I just wanted to be trusted with more. I do not always correct people if they do not call me Dr. Ashley, because I believe your work will always speak for itself. Those letters in front of your name starts the next journey in your life, but you have to be prepared.

Obtaining my degree was another step towards the legacy that I wanted to leave behind for my daughters and every other woman. Being in a male dominated career field and serving in the military creates a strength within that I could never explain. My purpose is to allow others to see that they can achieve their goals and there are ways to overcome. I held many roles and responsibilities during this journey, but I understood that if I worked hard now I could be in a better position later. We can enter rooms that were never meant for us based on what we can bring to the table, I strive to always be an asset to any team I am apart of and that is how you must think.

CHAPTER THIRTEEN:

The Morning After

"It was everything you wanted, now what do you do"

The high of graduating officially ended and then came feelings of uncertainty. Many people asked me what made me go to school or what did I plan to do with my degree, and I could never answer it. It was not because of the fact that I did not have a plan when I initially started my doctoral journey, but it was because I was already in a great career. I knew the military was going to be my end goal and for many on this journey, they are already in a good job. In order to retire from the United States Air Force, I am obligated to serve 10 more years and then I can retire, so the option to walk away and use my degree full time prior, never was an option. However, I am not misguided in understanding that you must use what you have earned, or it will be harder later to use.

Before you begin looking into what's next, take the time to enjoy your accomplishment. Take some time away from everyone and reassess if the goals that you had in the beginning of your program are still the same. Throughout your program you will be exposed to other opportunities and interests based on your courses and internships, so align your goals with where you are in your present state. Implement this assessment as a yearly routine, so find a system that works best for you and stick with it.

While I was in my program, I constantly updated my resume to make myself marketable. Another great tool that I found was casting my resume out to hiring officials and be prepared if my colleagues and peers had information on positions that I wanted to be considered for. Although I knew I did not meet all of the qualifications, I was able to receive constructive critiques in the following areas; interests that prospective jobs wanted on my resume, areas I should be administering my attention to, and developing connections for future employment opportunities.

Now it came down to a matter of, becoming purposeful in applying for jobs. Being in the military, I did not have the flexibility to apply for jobs outside of my geographical location unless it was an online position. I understood that I wanted to become an adjunct because this would allow me to stay in higher education, but in a part time capacity until I retire from the military. Not only did I know that I wanted to be an adjunct, but I was selective in the courses that I wanted to instruct as well. My educational background will allow me to teach a wide spectrum of classes, but it does not always mean that is where I need to be.

Discover where it is that you need to be. Never let the questions of what's next scare you, but let it fuel your drive. Now I find joy in mentoring young ladies and sharing my story with those that need an extra boost of encouragement. Regardless of our journeys, we all can get the "d".

APPENDIX A: PURPOSE BREAKDOWN

Write the top 3 purposes to each area category in your life and then beside it express the impact. Once you do this you will know your purpose and be reminded of the reason you are obtaining your doctorate.

Example: My purpose as a parent is to secure a job that will allow me to provide for my family and create generational wealth.

My purpose as a daughter/son:
1.
2.
3.
My purpose as a sibling:
1.
2.
3.
My purpose as a significant other:
1.
2.
3.
My purpose as a parent:
1.
2.

3.
My purpose as an employee/employer:
1.
2.
3.
My purpose as a friend:
1.
2.
3.

APPENDIX B: FINISHEDD/PHINISHED

1. Develop Educational and Career Goals

During this stage of your journey, you need to meet with your mentors and discuss what career plans that you want to pursue. While discussing your career plans, you will be provided with different options you can pursue in order to obtain your goals.

Make sure that you select the top two options in order to get the career that you want and then create a pros and cons chart for both options.

2. Select the Right School and Degree Program

There are many different options for you to receive your education to include in person, online, or hybrid. Ensure that regardless of the method you receive your education, you check the institution's accreditation and if there are any licensure steps that you will have to get prior to completion as well.

It is your responsibility to check the state requirements for the career path you are pursuing as well to make sure your program meets their requirements. If not, you may want to see if your school offers options to meet the state's requirements or what the state will let you do to waive/meet their requirement.

3. Secure Funding

When considering going back for your doctorate degree, many institutions offer fellowships and scholarships to pay for student's education. In return, the students may have to relocate among other requirements, but this is one option. You also want to reach out to the Human Resources (HR) Department within your company to see what benefits you are entitled to receive. Lastly, be mindful of completing your Free Application for Federal Student Aid (FASFA). It is best to complete this every October prior to the deadline so that you will be considered for federal grants, loans, and work-study funds.

4. Create Family Care Plans

Going back to college is an exciting time, but the excitement will fade once classes start and your family will need to be ready for the new shift of responsibility. Be transparent with your family about your new school obligation and identify roles that everyone will need to step into to prevent any areas of your home being neglected.

Develop a structured schedule that will still allow you time for your studies, but then find time to step away and devote time for your family. There will be moments when everyone must be flexible, but ensure that when it is family time, you make it memorable. Getting your doctorate degree effects everyone, especially children when they are used to having you whenever they want access to you.

5. Build a Strong Support System

Create a routine schedule where you check in with your close friends and family that are able to be a sounding board. The journey to receiving your doctorate degree will come with difficult days and you need someone that can listen to your difficult days and provide you clarity, while keeping you encouraged not to give up.

6. Remove Distractions

Limit things entering your space that are not helping you accomplish your goal. This could mean stepping away from social media because it is taking too much of your time or removing yourself from some circles of friends. If there are things in your life that are not keeping you encouraged or aligning with the direction you are going, they are distractions and you do not need them. Do not be afraid to protect your goals, regardless of what or whom you must separate from.

7. Work Smart

See what resources your school offers for free to assist with your assignments. There are many APA websites available and libraries that will allow you access to a multitude or literature for your assignments.

8. Rejuvenate

Never be afraid to just take self-time in order to bring balance to everything you are juggling. Enjoy doing things that bring you peace and also restore your mind and body. Maybe consider counseling, joining a workout group, or reading a book. Everyone needs something in their life that allows them time to focus on themselves.

APPENDIX C: APA HELPFUL SITES

Below is a list of helpful websites that provided assistance with my reference pages and APA formatting throughout my manuscript. There are other websites that work, but this is a great start while you're in your program. Also be mindful to check what reference sites your school may provide to you as well.

- *Easybib*

- *Bibme*

- *Citation Machine*

- *Citefast*

- *RefWorks (Strongly recommend due to the ability to create*

  multiple folders and reference page)

APPENDIX D: DISSERTATION/CAPSTONE KEY POINTS

The journey to becoming a doctor is not an overnight journey. Remember these key points below and always stay focused on what is ahead, not your present state.

- ☐ *Follow all instructions/examples of dissertations/capstones/IRB approvals verbatim*

- ☐ *Keep all verbiage consistent throughout your manuscript and all documentation*

- ☐ *Remove all ambiguity*

- ☐ *Create next step lists while waiting for formal review/edits/IRB approval*

- ☐ *Complete all edits from formal review/edits/IRB approval*

- ☐ *Schedule self time to focus on your physical and mental health*

- ☐ *Begin research upon formal review/edits/IRB approval*

- ☐ *Create a program specific checklist monthly and review it every week for progress*

www.ingramcontent.com/pod-product-compliance
Lightning Source LLC
Chambersburg PA
CBHW060157070426

42447CB00033B/2198